The Ten Commandments

LIVING GOD'S WAY

CWR

Mary Evans

Copyright © CWR 2011

Published 2011 by CWR, Waverley Abbey House, Waverley Lane, Farnham, Surrey GU9 8EP, UK. Registered Charity No. 294387. Registered Limited Company No. 1990308.

The right of Mary Evans to be identified as the author of this work has been asserted by her in accordance with the Copyright, Designs and Patents Act 1988, sections 77 and 78.

See back of book for list of National Distributors.

Unless otherwise indicated, all Scripture references are from the Holy Bible: New International Version (NIV), copyright © 1973, 1978, 1984 by the International Bible Society.
Other Scripture quotations are indicated as follows:
AV: Authorised Version
TNIV: Scripture taken from the HOLY BIBLE, TODAY'S NEW INTERNATIONAL VERSION®. Copyright © 2001, 2005 by Biblica®. Used by permission of Biblica®. All rights reserved worldwide.

Concept development, editing, design and production by CWR

Cover image: istock/JSP

Printed in the UK by Page Brothers, Norwich

ISBN: 978-1-85345-593-3

Contents

Introduction

Mention the Ten Commandments and virtually everyone, in the Western world at least, will know what you are talking about. They may not know the details, or even that they can be found in the Bible, but they will understand that you are referring to a set of moral principles that most people agree are a sensible basis for a good life. It can be a starting point for a good conversation. But often even Christians are a bit vague about exactly what the Ten Commandments contain and how or why they might be seen as relevant today, when because of what Jesus has done for us 'we are not under law but under grace' (Rom. 6:15). The seven studies in this book are intended to help us grasp both what these commandments meant in their original context and also what they can mean for us today as a dynamic and profoundly relevant section of God's living Word. Because they are so familiar, sometimes what we always thought they said and meant is not the same thing as what they actually do say. It is always worth looking very carefully at those passages of Scripture we think we know best. It is good, in addition, to point out that if you take these studies seriously it will also prove to be challenging and possibly even life-changing – so be warned! These certainly proved to be a challenging set of studies to write.

The Old Testament tells us that engraved on the stone tablets that God gave to Moses on Mount Sinai were 'The Ten Words' (Exod. 34:28; Deut. 4:1). Most English versions translate 'words' as 'commandments' and, although this is not the literal meaning of the Hebrew, it does help us to understand the sense. These were clearly intended to be a summary of the whole Law.

Often when we get a new computer, printer or some other electronic gadget, we are provided with a large handbook of detailed instructions. However, we also get a single-sheet list giving us a 'Quick-Start Guide' to help us get the general picture and use the machine straight away, before we have understood all its complexities. The 'Ten Words' function as this kind of 'Quick-Start Guide'. Of course for a full understanding of a new machine we do need to use the large handbook and we must never see the Ten Commandments as a replacement for the whole Bible – or even the whole Old Testament!

There are in fact several summaries of the Law, see for example the list in Leviticus 19. The teacher of the law in Luke 10:27 combined Deuteronomy 6:5 and Leviticus 19:18 to make an even shorter summary. However, although the text doesn't actually say so at any point, it is universally agreed that the 'Ten Words' refer to the list found in Exodus 20:2–17 and repeated in a slightly different form in Deuteronomy 5:6–21. The Deuteronomy list gives the fourth, fifth and tenth commandments in an expanded form but there is no difference at all in the basic sense or the obligations demanded. The original text contains no numbering and dividing the list up into ten parts is not quite as straightforward as it sounds. You may have noticed that Catholic and Protestant traditions, both referring to different scholars from the Early Church, have divided the commandments in a slightly different way. You can either see the Catholic list as joining the first two together and dividing the last one, or the Protestant list as dividing the first one and combining the last two. These studies have used the Protestant numbering but there is not necessarily a right or wrong answer to this. Both methods, in fact, see every element of the original as important.

Much of the Old Testament legal sections contain case-study laws (the technical term for this is casuistic law) – ie 'if this or that happens then you should take this or that action'. This does not necessarily mean that the original happening is good. As Jesus points out, the fact that the Law says 'if a man divorces his wife' followed by various regulations including giving her a certificate of divorce (eg Deut. 24:1–4), doesn't mean that God approves of divorce (Matt. 5:31–32). But, as well as the case studies there are command sections (the technical term is apodictic law) – ie 'you must do or not do this or that'. In these sections God's attitude to particular behaviour is very clear. The summaries, including the Ten Commandments come into the category of command law. The 'Ten Words' provide a basic summary of how Israel, as God's own covenant people, should live their lives. We need to be very clear from the beginning that this is not a 'pick your own' list! It is not a matter of getting a pass mark as long as we keep six out of ten. The list provides a whole picture and to fail in any one of the issues mentioned is to fail overall.

WEEK 1

Who Do You Think I Am?

Opening Icebreaker

Identify three things that you think would help other
people to understand who you are as a person – this may
be a physical characteristic, a character trait, something
that has happened to you or anything else you think
relevant. Go around the room (if there are too many
people, split up into groups) and introduce yourselves to
each other using these details.

Bible Readings

- Exodus 20:1–2
- Deuteronomy 4:1–6
- Exodus 3:13–15
- Isaiah 44:6,24–28
- Jeremiah 24:1–7
- John 15:1–8

Opening Our Eyes

The 'Ten Words' begin not with an instruction but with
an introduction. How many times have we as children,
when told to do something, replied: 'Why should I?' Many
reasons were given relating to how good it was for us,
or how it would help other people, but in the end the
one that really counted was 'Because I say so and I am
your mother/father/teacher ...!' Instructions given by bossy
brothers and sisters or 'interfering' strangers could be
responded to with the words: 'Why should I? You are *not*
my mother/father/teacher.' Rules must always be seen in
context. We keep laws because we belong to a community;
we follow customs because of the pressures and
expectations of our culture; we obey the rules of a club,
society or game because we've signed up to them etc.

The first words of Exodus 20 are not incidental. The
context they provide is vital to our understanding of the
whole passage. One of their functions is to remind us
that this is not just a collection of varying instructions
but a unified whole. You can't pick and choose which
commandments you will accept. They come as a package
deal. But, perhaps more significantly these Ten 'Words'
are God's words; if we forget that then we'll never be
able to understand the meaning of the commandments
themselves. Or, to put it another way, if we are to
understand God's words, we must first know who God
is and recognise our relationship to Him. Therefore
God begins by introducing Himself. He does this many
times throughout the Old Testament. When reading Old
Testament passages look out for it. We often hear of 'I am'
statements in the New Testament but they are also very
significant in the Old. Different forms of statements such
as 'I am the Lord', 'I am your God', 'I am your shield', 'I
am your inheritance' etc come more than two hundred
times. Here we have, 'I am the LORD your God ...'

When English versions spell LORD in capitals like this, it translates the name God gives Himself, Yahweh. (Sometimes 'Jehovah' is used, but this is a later formation taking the consonants of YHWH and combining them with vowels from another word meaning Lord.) God is not just an impersonal force. He is a Person with a name and He refers to Himself constantly by that name. There may have been good reasons for deciding to translate Yahweh by the title LORD, but we must never allow that tradition to stop us from grasping that God is a Person to whom we can relate and who relates to us. He is Yahweh, Israel's own God, the One who brought them 'out of Egypt, out of the land of slavery'.

God is saying to Israel: 'Listen folks, it really is Me speaking here. We have a history together. You used to be slaves in Egypt but I rescued you. You have signed up to the covenant with Me, so I am "your God". We belong together. Because of that I am giving you these Ten 'Words' as the foundational basis for how life should be lived in the new land I am giving you. It is Me who is giving you these words and "because I say so" you must keep them.' The reason for obeying the Ten Commandments is that they come from our God and tell us something of the kind of things this God of ours requires.

Discussion Starters

1. 'And God spoke all these words ...' (Exod. 20:1). Have you heard from God recently either in Scripture or otherwise? If so how did He speak and what did you hear?

_____

_____

_____

_____

2. What difference, if any, does it make when we call people by their name or by a title? (In some cultures similar differences might apply if we use the first name or the family name.)

_____

_____

_____

_____

3. Some modern English translations (eg Jerusalem Bible) are beginning to use the name Yahweh instead of replacing it with LORD. Is this a good or a bad thing?

_____

_____

_____

_____

4. In general, when you speak to God what do you call Him? Does what you call Him make any difference to your relationship with Him? If you begin, for example, with 'Loving heavenly Father', how might the prayer following that differ from a prayer beginning 'Great Creator and Lord of the whole universe'?

_____

_____

_____

_____

5. God uses different aspects of His character or blessings when He speaks of Himself to Israel. Here it is redemption from Egypt; sometimes (eg Jer. 34:13) it is as the Giver of the covenant, or as the God of their ancestors. What things do you think God might mention if He were introducing Himself to

a) your country?

_____
_____
_____
_____

b) your church?

_____
_____
_____
_____

c) you?

_____
_____
_____
_____

6. How does our understanding of who God is affect our understanding of what we think it means for us to serve Him?

_____
_____
_____
_____

Personal Application

Any meaningful relationship always involves both behaviour and knowledge. Of course love must be evidenced by loving behaviour, but how many relationships founder because they are based on a mirage? Love based on what we think the other person should be like, rather than the reality, does not usually last long. God knows all about us and loves us anyway, but do we really take time to discover who God is, to listen to what He says about Himself in His Word? In the following studies we will discuss our attitudes and actions in relation to God. But if that is to have any relevance we must first know to whom we are relating. Take time to write down some things you know about God and make a note of Scripture verses providing evidence that what you 'know' is correct. Try using a different name or title for God each time you pray this week and see how this affects the way you think about Him.

Seeing Jesus in the Scriptures

Jesus said, 'I and the Father are one' (John 10:30) and 'Anyone who has seen me has seen the Father' (John 14:9). When we look at Jesus we also learn things about the Father. However, we must realise that when God speaks about Himself in the Old Testament we also learn more about Jesus. Relationship with God and relationship with Jesus are not two completely separate things but are linked together. Yahweh as Israel's Redeemer in Exodus 20:2 helps us understand more of the New Testament's presentation of Christ as Redeemer – and vice versa.

WEEK 2

Exclusive Rights

Opening Icebreaker

Many shops and businesses today issue 'loyalty cards' or give a 'loyalty bonus'. Talk about the expectations that this creates on both sides. Can you think of other situations where you expect people to show loyalty to you or they expect you to show loyalty to them?

Bible Readings

- Exodus 20:3–6
- Deuteronomy 4:15–20,35–40; 6:4–7
- Isaiah 43:1–13
- Mark 12:28–34

Opening Our Eyes

Now Yahweh has introduced Himself, the ground rules for ongoing covenant relationship begin to be made clear. The people of Israel must first grasp that their God is unique and incomparable.

The emphasis in the first 'Word' (Exod. 20:3; Deut. 5:7) is that God is uniquely to be served – just as the first ground rule for marriage is exclusivity, or for sponsorship of events that only the sponsor's products are sold. However, Deuteronomy 6:4 makes it clear that understood within God's demands for exclusive service is His own uniqueness. Nations surrounding Israel almost universally worshipped many gods: their pantheons were complex and divided. But Israel must understand that this does not reflect reality. 'Yahweh our God, Yahweh is One' means both that there is only one God and that there is one-ness within God. Firstly, Yahweh alone is God. The command to 'have no other gods' does not imply that other gods exist. Biblical faith is not just monolatry (worship of only one God), it is monotheism – the recognition that there is only one God to be worshipped. Isaiah's majestic arguments in chapters 40–45 of his book make this abundantly clear. Secondly, God is one, He is not divided. New Testament teaching which links the Father, the Son and the Holy Spirit (eg Matt. 28:19) and was explained in the Early Church in terms of the doctrine of the Trinity does not contradict the essential oneness within the godhead. Christians must be very careful not to give the impression that when we speak of God as three-in-one, this somehow diminishes His oneness or that there is or could be any difference of purpose or intention between the different persons of the Trinity. And this one, unique God must be served exclusively. Loyalty to Him must be absolute. In terms of our worship and service, nothing must replace Him or be added to Him. Pledging allegiance to any kind of other god is the equivalent of issuing divorce papers to Yahweh. Under those circumstances the covenant no longer exists.

God's incomparability also comes out in the second commandment that they are to make and to serve no images. Any image that human beings themselves create is not and should never be seen as an image of Yahweh. However well-intentioned such creations might be, bowing down to an image counts as bowing down to another god and Yahweh cannot and will not tolerate this amongst His people. Deuteronomy 4:15–19 expands this concept. Using verbal imagery to describe God is common throughout Scripture and clearly not seen as wrong. God is pictured for example as a shepherd (Psa. 23), a soldier (Exod. 15:3), a mother (Isa. 66:13) or a lion (Isa. 31:4), but there is always recognition that this language is metaphorical. These are pictures not definitions. Most of us are unlikely to sculpt any image and call it God, but perhaps we are in danger of creating mental images. Do we imagine God as an animal, bird, fish or star? Probably not; but do we picture God as a female or, more likely, a male? Deuteronomy 4:16 warns us against this as well. Exodus 20:5–6 (Deut. 5:9–10) is sometimes seen as contradicting Deuteronomy 24:16, which unambiguously teaches that punishment does not cross generations. But the point here is that every generation that hates God (apparently evidenced by worshipping images) deserves punishment. Parental teaching does influence children but this is not inevitable. The difference between the three or four and the thousand is meant to emphasise the extent of God's love.

Discussion Starters

1. If God were to give you a loyalty card, what would you expect to give and to get?

_____

_____

_____

_____

2. If you were to give God a loyalty card, what would you expect to give and to get?

_____

_____

_____

_____

3. Are there any aspects of our lives where we owe or expect exclusive loyalty? Think about how you might feel if you were betrayed by someone who owes you such loyalty. Does this help us to understand how God might feel when He is betrayed?

_____

_____

_____

_____

4. What people, things or ideas might be likely to draw us away from exclusive worship of God? Is there any action we can take to avoid this danger?

_____

_____

_____

_____

5. People today are very wary of absolute claims. How do you understand the Bible's teaching about the uniqueness of God, and how does this actually affect the way you live your life?

_____

_____

_____

_____

6. Jesus said, 'I and the Father are one' (John 10:30). Talk about how we can understand this unity of the Father, the Son and the Holy Spirit.

_____

_____

_____

_____

7. Medieval paintings almost invariably picture God as an old man with a white beard. Is there anything wrong with this?

_____

_____

_____

_____

8. Do you have a mental picture of God? Is there any danger of this picture becoming a definition of God for you rather than an illustration of some aspect or aspects of God's character?

_____

_____

_____

_____

Personal Application

One of the biggest barriers to giving exclusive allegiance to God is our failure to identify the 'gods' we are really serving. We all know that commercialism, money and the love of money are major problems in modern society, but it is easy to assume that because we are not the richest in our social group, or we give more to charity than others do, we have avoided the problem. Or we hide behind the excuse of: 'We are doing this for the family'. But do our children really need the latest i-gadget, or designer trainers, or even the 'best' education? Indeed has education in itself become a 'god' for us? Has obtaining this or that certificate or degree become the primary goal in life for either ourselves or for our children? Or is it reaching a particular level of promotion so that, in our heart of hearts, we look down on others (or on ourselves) if that level is not reached? The answers will be different for all of us, but it is worth asking ourselves what is our greatest ambition for ourselves or for our families – and whether or where God comes into the picture.

Seeing Jesus in the Scriptures

No humanly created image, whether mental or physical, can adequately represent God. But Colossians 1:15 reminds us that '[The Son] is the image of the invisible God ...'. We can test the accuracy of any picture or idea we have of God by asking whether or not that idea is reflected in Jesus.

WEEK 3

Misrepresentation

Opening Icebreaker

Have a look at some TV adverts or, if that is not possible, large magazine adverts where the name of the product can be cut out. Ask yourself or discuss within the group what the film clips or the pictures are implying and what they might tell us about the product involved. Is it always possible to guess the product from the advertisement?

Bible Readings

- Exodus 20:7
- Deuteronomy 32:1–4
- 1 Kings 8:20–30
- Proverbs 18:10
- Ezekiel 36:16–32
- Philippians 2:9–11

Opening Our Eyes

Over the last couple of nights watching TV in Australia (including UK and US programmes) I have heard God's name used many times both in dramas and on live TV, by adults and children. Sometimes used negatively, expressing violence or fear or bad feelings about people, sometimes positively to express wonder or joy. But, excluding filming in Christian services, only once, when a little girl progressing to the next stage of a cooking competition looked up and said, 'Thank You, God', was there any sign of the speakers having any idea what they were saying or of whom they were speaking. Almost always, there would have been no thought of giving offence. The name of Almighty God has become a mild form of meaningless swearing. Should we be offended that God's name has been misused or, as the AV puts it, used 'in vain' (ie emptied of meaning) in this way? I think we should! It is clear that the 'name of the LORD', the 'name of Yahweh' is used synonymously with Yahweh Himself. Calling on or praising the name of the LORD is calling on or praising the LORD. To use God's name thoughtlessly suggests that God is of no account: this insults God and should be seen as insulting by God's people. Because this has become so common in modern language Christians must be particularly careful not to use God's name in such a way.

Growing up in a Christian family I used to think that this was an easy commandment to keep. I was not used to hearing swearing, and it would never have entered my head to use God's name as part of thoughtless conversation. It just wasn't a temptation, so I could tick that one off very easily. However, I have realised that actually this is one of the easiest commandments to break. This is not because hearing God's name misused so often influences us but because that casual usage, though offensive, is actually not the worst offence. Ezekiel 36 makes it very clear that God's name is profaned when God's people misrepresent Him. Israel were the people of Yahweh. Surrounding nations were supposed to learn something of who Yahweh was by observing His people. When Israel tolerated injustice or practised idolatry they were saying to the nations: 'God doesn't care about this' – when He most certainly did. To profane God's name was to proclaim, by action as well as by word, untruths about the God whose name they bore. And God really cares that people know who He is. One of the key reasons God called Israel to be His own people was so that they could represent Him. Ezekiel tells us that a prime reason for the exile was that God wanted the nations to be sure that He was not the kind of God who tolerated Israel's behaviour. However that might lead outsiders to think that Israel's God was not powerful, so one of the main reasons for their redemption was also that outsiders would understand that God is powerful in and over all nations.

Every Christian bears Christ's name and people look at us, what we do more than what we say, and draw conclusions about what Christ is like. Every time we behave in a way that dishonours or displeases Jesus, we are misrepresenting Him to our neighbours, therefore misusing His name. Not swearing is good, but the only way to keep this commandment is to reflect Jesus in all that we do.

Discussion Starters

1. How does it make you feel if you hear God's name misused? Does it really matter if the people involved don't mean to be offensive?

_____

_____

_____

2. Why do you think the use of the name of God or of Jesus as a thoughtless exclamation has become so common? Can you think of any ways that Christians could use this as a means of bringing their own knowledge of God into the conversation without sounding judgmental about the speaker?

_____

_____

_____

3. Is it true that if Christians used God's name in a good way more often, then others would misuse His name less?

_____

_____

_____

4. Most common exclamations seem to be either blasphemous or making unpleasant reference to bodily functions. These are all clearly unacceptable. Are there alternative acceptable exclamations when, for example, you drop a hammer on your foot, or should Christians always restrict themselves to a simple 'Ow!'?

_____

_____

_____

5. Talk about situations where you have known people to get the wrong impression of God because of the way Christians behave.

_____

_____

_____

6. Make no. 5 above personal. Is there anything relating to my behaviour over the last week that might have given people the wrong impression about Jesus? Could the way in which my church functions or interacts give people the wrong impression about Jesus? Do I recognise my part in that – or is it always someone else's fault?

_____

_____

_____

7. As a group (or on your own) write out a prayer that you could use now asking God to help you to avoid misusing His name. You may like to make a commitment to pray this prayer for each other during the coming week.

_____

_____

_____

8. Do you think that if the first three commandments were properly kept then the rest would all actually be included within that?

_____

_____

_____

Personal Application

The huge challenge each one of us faces is this: to avoid misusing God's name by claiming that we belong to Him and yet behaving in a way that dishonours or misrepresents Him. We may be able to avoid using the name of God thoughtlessly in speech, but can we avoid dishonouring God in our actions? We certainly need His help here. It means constantly asking myself whether, if I am taking a particular course of action, anyone looking on would be right in assuming that God must approve of it! Maybe each time we pray the Lord's Prayer, we should remember that God's name is 'hallowed' or considered as holy, when His will is done on earth – by me – as it is in heaven.

 ## Seeing Jesus in the Scriptures

There is only one human being who has ever spent His whole life representing as well as reflecting God properly, and that is Jesus. He shows us by His example what it means to live in the way God intended. It is comforting to know that He is also the One who provides the means for us to do so, not only by taking our sin and giving us His righteousness, but by asking the Father to send us His Spirit. Read John 14:15–17.

WEEK 4

Respect!

Opening Icebreaker

On a piece of paper, write down the names of all the people in the group. By each name put down one thing about that person (including yourself) that you think is particularly worthy of respect. Swap the lists round (so that no one knows who wrote which list) and read them out.

Bible Readings

- Exodus 20:8–12
- Deuteronomy 5:12–16
- Nehemiah 13:15–22
- Mark 2:27–3:6
- Genesis 2:23–24
- Matthew 15:1–9

Opening Our Eyes

'Respect!' has become a key watchword amongst young people in the twenty-first century, particularly amongst those who see themselves as in some way disenfranchised. The point they are making seems to be that they should receive the respect of others, sometimes suggesting that if this is not given they will take action to ensure that it is. The Respect media campaign developed this idea without the negative connotations but is still concerned with respect for rather than from the people involved.

The Bible, using various terms, also talks a lot about respect, both for institutions, like the Sabbath, and for people, like parents. It agrees with the young people's concept that people do deserve respect. However the emphasis is very different. The stress is not on the respect you should demand from others but on the respect you yourselves should give.

a) Respect the Sabbath. The reasons given in Exodus and Deuteronomy to back up this command are different. Exodus 20 bases it on the fact that God rested on the seventh day of creation whereas Deuteromony 5 uses Israel's deliverance from Egypt and the fact that they were all once slaves. Later on, the emphasis on the Sabbath became more focused on rituals and this was seen as a particularly suitable day for worshipping God – Jesus attended the synagogue regularly on Sabbath days (Luke 4:16). But the Ten Words themselves focus on the Sabbath as a time of relaxation and leisure. One day in every seven, work should be put aside. The creation argument tells us that this was part of God's plan from the very beginning, for all people, not just for Israel. Human beings have been created with the need for rest and God Himself stands as an example to them. To ignore this command is to disrespect God – not to speak of risking burnout! To argue that if I don't work seven days this week then the crops might not be gathered in, or the essay might not be written, or the contract not completed is usually to say that I have taken on too much or not used my time properly – but it also says that I don't trust God. And in addition we have a responsibility to respect the right of others to rest. We must make sure that all those for whom we have responsibility, whether family or employees, humans or working animals, are given and take up that right.

b) Respect your parents. As Paul points out (Eph. 6:2), this is the first commandment with a promise. Deuteronomy, with its focus on what it means to live in the God-provided land as God's covenant people, expands on both the instruction and the promise. For a society to function in the best way possible then good family life is crucial. Children giving respect to parents is a key element of this and a society where this happens is likely to be long lasting. Genesis 2:24 makes it clear that the honour to be given to parents is not without limits, and responsibility to a spouse takes priority, but this does not remove, even for adult children, the need to respect parents. Paul, speaking specifically of children not adults, uses the word 'obey', but it is perhaps significant that the Old Testament does not use that word in this context – although obedience to parents may often be relevant and required in order to show respect. Note that the respect is to be given equally to both father and mother. Where the Bible speaks of parental responsibilities and rights it very rarely makes a distinction between father and mother.

Discussion Starters

1. Is observing/remembering the Sabbath the same thing as 'keeping Sunday special'? Discuss the reasons behind your answer.

2. 'Working all the hours that God sends' is often seen as a sign of Christian commitment rather than the sin the Bible presents it to be. Why do you think this is?

3. Talk about the things – other than your paid work – that you enjoy doing. Which of these do you think is or is not appropriate to do on your Sabbath day? What difference might it make if someone has retired from their paid work – should they still have a Sabbath day?

4. The New Testament is insistent that meeting together as Christians for worship and fellowship is vital. Is this the same thing as keeping the Sabbath?

5. Will the way to respect one's parents (Lev. 19:3) be different in different cultures? What do you think it means in your culture?

_____

_____

_____

_____

6. How might honouring parents be different for children who have or have not 'come of age'?

_____

_____

_____

_____

7. Is honouring elderly parents the same thing as looking after them? What does it mean to honour or respect those who are suffering from dementia?

_____

_____

_____

_____

8. Do parents ever make unreasonable demands on their children based on this commandment? How could or should the church advise both parties if they see this happening?

_____

_____

_____

_____

Personal Application

The application of either or both of these commandments will be very different depending on our age and stage of life. If the Sunday service is an oasis for us and the whole day is calm and relaxed then that could be our Sabbath. On the other hand, if we are very involved in church work and Sunday is spent in a constant rush then we should almost certainly take another day. Do we make sure that our children have a special day – perhaps a day away from the computer? And if someone runs our household do we make sure that they get a day away from the cooking and washing up? Those with parents might like to make a special commitment this week to do something special to honour them. For those who have no living parents the fifth commandment might seem irrelevant, but it is worth us all asking whether or not we give proper respect to all those in our life who have cared for us or to whom we owe a duty of care.

Seeing Jesus in the Scriptures

Jesus again provides us an example in relation to both these commandments. He is seen as attending the synagogue on the Sabbath and as honouring His parents (Luke 4:16; 2:51; John 19:26–27). However, He did not see the expectations of His culture as controlling His behaviour on the Sabbath (Luke 13:10–17; Mark 2:23–27; John 7:22–23) and respect for His parents did not prevent Him acting on His own initiative – even at the age of twelve.

WEEK 5

Sex and Violence

Opening Icebreaker

Make a list of at least three things belonging to you that you would most hate to be taken from you. Compare your list with those of others and pick out the three things that you, as a group, agree to be the most significant.

Bible Readings

- Exodus 20:13–15; 21:12–27
- Genesis 9:1–6
- 2 Samuel 12:1–10
- John 8:1–11
- Proverbs 30:7–9

Opening Our Eyes

Every human society throughout the world and throughout the ages seems to have agreed that murder, adultery and theft are wrong. They may understand the terms slightly differently; for example there are a few cultures where the concept of personal property does not seem to exist, but these are rare, and even there for one village to take what belongs to another village is usually seen as wrong. All these commandments relate to the taking away of something that belongs not to you, but to someone else.

a) There is something special about life! Whether it is defined in terms of breath, or of consciousness, or in any other way, there is no doubt that life is precious. It is precious not just to the person who possesses it, but in and of itself. The Bible presents life as both given by God and belonging to God. This concept is expressed symbolically for Israel by not eating blood, which was seen as the bearer of life. All life is God's, but humanity is made in the image of God and human life is particularly valuable (Gen. 9:5–6). To take away the life of another human being is hugely significant. It is to take something that belongs not just to the person involved but to God. It is clear that there are certain instances within the Old Testament, in war, or as part of the justice system, when the taking of life seems to have been sanctioned by God, but even here it is never to be taken lightly. Any society which treats human life as insignificant is a society going against God's purposes for humankind and probably on the verge of collapse.

b) The Bible is not unrealistic – it recognises that marriage is not always ideal (Prov. 21:9). However marriage is always presented, like life, as being special. The relationship between husband and wife is pictured as closer and more significant than that between a child and their parents (Gen. 2:24). In ancient times adultery was almost always seen as a crime against a husband, but Jesus makes it clear that any man taking another woman commits adultery against his wife. To take someone else's spouse and treat them as if they were your own is to destroy the marriage relationship – and God sees this as completely unacceptable. Marriage is the foundation of family life, and family life is the foundation of society. Any society which begins to treat marriage as insignificant is a society going against God's purposes for humankind and probably on of the verge of collapse.

c) Stealing is a little harder to define because property, ownership and rights can be understood in different ways. It is clear that taking what belongs to someone else is wrong; theft from someone's home, pocket or shop, or from one's employer all come into this category. But prophets like Amos and Micah make it clear that other things are also condemned: for example, denying justice to those without power; not paying fair wages; using unbalanced scales; or even foreclosing on a loan when it would involve making a poor person destitute. Any society that does not properly identify and acknowledge the ownership rights of all its citizens is a society going against God's purposes for humankind and probably on the verge of collapse.

Discussion Starters

1. Most modern versions interpret 'you shall not kill' as 'you shall not murder'. Are they right to do so? Spend some time thinking about how this commandment may or may not relate to the death penalty, abortion, euthanasia or suicide.

_____

_____

_____

2. Should any lack of concern for human life, eg drinking and driving, smoking when others are present, speeding or ignoring other safety regulations, or even risking our own life by over- or undereating, be seen as breaking the sixth commandment?

_____

_____

_____

3. 'As long as no one finds out, then no one gets hurt' and 'We loved one another so it must be all right' are used to excuse adultery in many modern societies. Can these ever be seen as valid excuses?

_____

_____

_____

4. Why is marriage so important? What difference do you really think it will make to a society when the proportion of people getting married steadily decreases and the proportion of those living together outside of marriage rapidly increases?

_____

_____

_____

5. What does or could your church do to strengthen the appreciation of the value of marriage amongst young people?

_____

_____

_____

6. Can you think of anything that happens in your business, local community, family or church that might be seen as stealing something that belongs to somebody else?

_____

_____

_____

7. Modern international business practices, trade restrictions, and sometimes even aid payments which are given with strings attached, often favour big companies over small companies and developed countries over developing countries. Does the eighth commandment have any relevance to this?

_____

_____

_____

8. There is no doubt that murder, adultery and theft are wrong. But what should be the Christian attitude to those who are found to have offended? Will this be any different from the general attitude of society?

_____

_____

_____

Personal Application

For most law-abiding Christians it is very easy to see these commandments as only relevant to us when others break them! But perhaps we should all take a 'health check' every now and then relating to our own attitudes and behaviour. How far does my own respect for human life stretch? Does it include those from other communities or in other countries? Do I respect those severely disabled as much as those without obvious disabilities? Does my respect for human life affect my behaviour towards other people or is not actually murdering anyone else enough? How far does my respect for marriage stretch? Does it include supporting the marriages of others, making sure that nothing I do or say creates dissension between spouses, or is not sleeping with someone's spouse enough? How far does my respect for what others own stretch? Does it involve concern for their rights and needs or is simply not stealing their property enough?

Seeing Jesus in the Scriptures

Jesus apparently saw the keeping of these commandments as an important pre-requisite for anybody who wants to 'inherit eternal life' (Matthew 19:18; Mark 10:19; Luke 18:20). His attitude towards those who failed to keep them was sometimes more merciful than that of some Jewish leaders of His time but He did not disagree with their conviction that these rules should be followed.

WEEK 6

Who Are You Kidding?

Opening Icebreaker

Take a number from the box and, in turn, according to that number, select and open a gift. If you would prefer a gift that has already been opened by someone else, you can swap yours for theirs (but without talking to them). When everyone has opened (and finished swapping) their gifts, discuss how this exercise made you feel.

Bible Readings

- Exodus 20:16–17;
- Proverbs 19:5; 21:28; 25:18: 26:18–19
- Isaiah 29:19–21

- Ephesians 4:14–21
- Deuteronomy 5:20–21
- Micah 2:1–5
- James 4:1–3

Opening Our Eyes

There are several instructions within the Old Testament legal sections speaking of responsibility towards neighbours. These are usually assumed to be fellow Israelites living nearby, although of course Jesus' discussion with the legal expert (Luke 10:25–37) expands on this definition. The last two commandments pick out two of these specific responsibilities. However, Leviticus 19:18 '... love your neighbour as yourself', also used by Jesus, show that these responsibilities do go much wider than the two examples given here.

a) It may not always seem like it today, but all legal systems are dedicated to finding out the truth. Doing that is almost always dependent on the testimony of witnesses. Therefore giving false testimony not only damages the individual concerned, it opens cracks in the whole system. It destroys not only truth but trust, and both of these are fundamental to the wellbeing of any society and, in particular, its justice system. This is why giving false testimony is often known as 'contempt of court' and is treated very seriously indeed. The primary concern here is almost certainly with the court case scenario but the concepts of truth and trust involved go far beyond that. That Yahweh can be trusted is affirmed constantly throughout Scripture: it lies at the heart of Israel's covenant relationship with Him. Truth, too, is a fundamental aspect of God's nature seen throughout the Bible. Anyone who claims to follow God must be trustworthy and truthful in every aspect of their life. The right to privacy has become a given in Western society and confidentiality is seen as a primary virtue. Other societies sometimes take it for granted that information about community members is public property and the Western concept of privacy is incomprehensible. But in both instances it is absolutely vital that any information shared should be correct. Even outside the courts, false testimony is unacceptable.

b) There are many pressures and expectations on us today. Peer pressure, often controlled by commercial interests, tells us that we must have this phone, wear these clothes, buy this furniture or drink this drink. Sometimes this pressure is dressed up in seemingly good value judgments – we must send our children to this kind of school and give them this kind of holiday or that kind of present. But it is very easy for this to turn into coveting what our neighbour has. Coveting has two aspects. On the one hand, craving for what others have is in itself problematic because it leads to discontent or jealousy. But, secondly, coveting also involves wishing that we, instead of they, owned certain things. And, as we see when Ahab desired Naboth's vineyard (1 Kings 21) or in Micah 2:1–2, the step between coveting and taking is not a long one. But, even if we don't have the power to take (Micah 2:1), coveting is still disrespecting not only our neighbour but also both God and ourselves: God, by suggesting that His provision for us is not adequate; and ourselves, by failing to recognise the value in who we are and what we have. In today's terms the commandment says: 'Don't long that your neighbour's spouse could be yours. Don't get yourself in a state over how much richer she or he is, or how much bigger and better is their property or their business. And don't even think about wishing their car was really yours. In fact accept them as they are for what they have and learn to be content with your own situation' (cf. Phil. 4:11).

Discussion Starters

1. Leviticus 19:11 condemns all kinds of deceit not just false testimony. Does this mean that lying is always wrong?

_____

_____

_____

_____

2. When the Bible uses the term gossip, it usually means passing on negative information about someone (Prov. 26:20,22; 2 Cor. 12:20). Is all talk about other people unacceptable, or only that which is either wrong or negative?

_____

_____

_____

_____

3. Discuss times when you have heard or passed on information that later turned out to be incorrect. Does this matter? How important is it to check what we have heard before we pass it on?

_____

_____

_____

_____

4. Is there a difference between false testimony that causes someone to be wrongly convicted and false testimony that stops someone from being convicted? Does it make a difference whether the latter person was actually guilty or innocent?

_____

_____

_____

_____

5. Discuss how far advertising campaigns increase the temptation for us to covet. Is it wrong to buy something just because someone we admire already has it?

_____

_____

_____

_____

6. Peer pressure is very strong. How can a) parents and b) the church equip children to deal with the phenomenon of 'Keeping up with the Joneses'? Is our 'natural' desire for our children (or grandchildren) to have the best actually part of the phenomenon?

_____

_____

_____

_____

7. What more would you need to make you content with what you have?

_____

_____

_____

_____

8. 'Passing thoughts can't be helped but allowing those thoughts to take root in your mind is your own responsibility.' Is this true – and does it have relevance to the commandment about coveting?

_____

_____

_____

_____

Personal Application

We are all tempted in different ways and by different things. Those who are not interested in other people are not tempted to talk about them – but is this necessarily a good thing? There are always grey areas but, in general, I think we all know when our talk is generous and good-hearted and when it is unkind or revelling in someone else's difficulties or failures. Sometimes when we've heard only one side of a story we can get a false impression. If we pass this on, or allow this impression to influence other people, it could be seen as giving false testimony. I think also we all know the difference between a generous-hearted appreciation of what someone else has and a jealous or greedy desire to have it for ourselves. This week, take a few minutes each evening to look back over the day and consider whether, for you, either false testimony or coveting has been a part of it. Talk to God about your conclusions.

Seeing Jesus in the Scriptures

Jesus said 'I am ... the truth ...' (John 14:6). John's Gospel constantly stresses truth and how important a concept it is for Jesus. He sends us 'the Spirit of truth' (16:13) and calls us to testify to the truth. His word is truth. Truth-telling seems to be a vital ingredient for those who are called to speak of 'the Truth'. Matthew 8:20 and 19:21–23 tell us something of Jesus' attitude to possessions. If He called me to give up ..., would I still want to follow Him?

WEEK 7

The Now Generation

Opening Icebreaker

Take ten years off the approximate average age of the group. Working as a group, make a list of things that have remained the same and things that have changed over that number of years, firstly in schools and then in churches.

Bible Readings

- Matthew 5:17–48
- Matthew 19:16–25
- Mark 12:28–34
- Luke 10:25–37
- Romans 7:1–6
- Romans 13:8–10

Opening Our Eyes

The New Testament says far too much about the Ten Commandments for us to consider in just one study. Many who came to question Jesus wanted to discuss the Law, and sometimes He introduces the topic. Paul's writings constantly expound the relationship between law and faith in relation to salvation, and James could be seen as an extended discussion of how the Ten Commandments relate to Christians. So let us consider just three areas.

1. The heart of the Law

Both Jesus (Mark 12:30) and the legal expert (Luke 10:27) gave the same answer as to the most important commandment. They didn't mention the Ten Commandments, but combined Deuteronomy 6:4–5 and Leviticus 19:18 as summarising what is required. In order to 'live' one must love God totally with every aspect of your being and 'love your neighbour as yourself'. This is seen to adequately summarise all the Ten Commandments (eg Matt. 19:16–19; Rom. 13:9). Note that they are quoting from the Old Testament. This is how the Law was always meant to be understood: if you love God and love your neighbour then keeping the other commandments follows automatically. The Ten Commandments were simply specific illustrations of what loving God and neighbour meant for Israel.

2. Jesus reinterprets the Law

In the Sermon on the Mount, particularly Matthew 5, Jesus seems to go beyond the Law. He explains that it isn't just murder or adultery that breaks God's commandments (and at the same time breaks God's heart), but anger and lust as well. It really was the thought that counted! The religious leaders had worked out exactly what actions did and did not break the Law, sometimes including how they could get round the obvious meaning (cf Mark 7:8–13).

But for Jesus keeping the Law was not about how little we must do to satisfy God, but how much we can do to please Him. Jesus is not so much changing the Law itself, although He is changing the accepted interpretation of it, but expressing what it was always meant to be. The story of the adulterous woman (John 7:53–8:11; which was added later to John's Gospel, but there is no real reason to doubt its historicity) shows Jesus recognising that adultery was wrong, but asserting that showing mercy was not alien to the spirit of the Law (cf Psalm 51 where God shows mercy to David even though he had broken the Law).

3. Freedom from the Law

In Romans 7, Paul explains that because Christ has fulfilled the Law those who trust in Him have been freed from it. This freedom does not mean that Christians can do what they like, rather they are free to 'bear fruit for God' (v.4, TNIV) and to 'serve in the new way of the Spirit' (v.6). We should behave in godly ways, not because the Law says so, but because it is right and pleases God. The Law was given to explain how the nation of Israel should function. Some rules only apply in that context. However, the Ten Commandments remain good illustrations of the kind of things that do and do not please God. It is interesting that each of the commandments except the fourth is clearly reaffirmed within the New Testament. However it is not obvious whether clear reaffirmation of the Sabbath rule is missing because it only applied within Israel or because it had been applied in such a twisted way that it would have been impossible for readers to understand properly.

Discussion Starters

1. What is the same and what is different about the New Testament and the Old Testament views of the Law?

_____

_____

_____

_____

2. It seems a contradiction in terms for the New Testament to state that the Law no longer applies to us as Christians yet certain elements of the Law still seem to be required. How can we make sense of this?

_____

_____

_____

_____

3. The religious leaders of Jesus' day had turned legalism into an art form. Talk about areas where we might be in danger of doing the same thing today.

_____

_____

_____

_____

4. Why do you think that the Sabbath laws are not re-emphasised within the New Testament when all the other nine commandments are? Does this mean that we can ignore the requirement to rest?

_____

_____

_____

_____

5. Spend some time thinking about how each of the Ten Commandments fits in with wholeheartedly loving God and our neighbour.

_____

_____

_____

_____

6. Is there anything in a) your church life or b) your family life which, although not strictly breaking one of the Ten Commandments, could be seen as not evidencing wholehearted love?

_____

_____

_____

_____

7. Make a list of specific illustrations as to how wholeheartedly loving God and your neighbour might apply in your society (ie commandments for today). How different might the list be if it was directed to young people, old people or those in between?

_____

_____

_____

_____

Personal Application

It is not always easy to get the balance right between, on the one hand, making sure that everything I do is right and brings glory to God and, on the other hand, really understanding what it means for me to have freedom from the Law. We know that keeping the commandments will in no way bring us salvation. But we also know that keeping what James calls the 'royal law' (James 2:8), (that is, loving our neighbour as ourselves – with all that that includes), provides important evidence that we have received salvation. Legalism is out, but fruitful loving service is in! It seems to be as much a matter of attitude as anything else. When I do the right thing, is it because I have a wonderful sense of freedom and a deep desire to serve God out of thankfulness and love? Or rather is it because I feel a sense of burden and guilt? Maybe we should ask God each day to help us know joy and freedom as we seek to bear fruit for Him.

Seeing Jesus in the Scriptures

Looking at the way in which Jesus affirms the commandments but clearly sees them as reflecting a living truth and relationship (rather than in the context of a dry legalism) may, perhaps, provide a way forward for us too. His death and resurrection bring us freedom *from* the Law. Maybe we should also see His life of obedience to God bringing us freedom *in* the Law.

Leader's Notes

It may seem excessive to spend seven weeks studying just one fairly short passage of Scripture but the Ten Commandments have played a uniquely significant role in the life of both Israel and the Church. I hope you will find the effort of this fairly intensive study well repaid. It is important to set these verses in the context of the whole of the Bible. There are several passages suggested for each study but most of these are fairly short. It would be helpful if everyone in the group has read all the passages in advance but you may like to assign each passage particularly to one person in the group in order that the person can think in advance how their passage might relate to the section of the Ten Commandments under consideration that week.

Week 1: Who Do You Think I Am?

Opening Icebreaker

The Opening Icebreaker is intended to stimulate the group to think about what it means to know someone else. If the group know each other really well, then suggest that they all try to think of at least one thing that the rest might not know about them. If the majority of items come in the same category, eg physical characteristics or family relationships ('I am the mother/ husband/daughter/... of') then get the group to ask why this might be and to discuss what it is about ourselves that best describes who we are. In a talkative group this exercise can go on for a long time and you might need to draw it to a close after a few minutes.

Aim of the Session

The aim of this study is to get across the point that the Ten Commandments start with God, not with us. They tell us about who God is, how God relates to us and what God wants and expects from us. Yes, they are about our behaviour, but only in the context of our relationship with God as He really is, rather than as we might imagine Him to be. Unless we grasp this point we won't understand the actual requirements and we certainly won't be able to keep them. It will be easy for the group to move away from this point in all the studies and it will be helpful if you can keep reminding them of it as the different commandments are considered.

Discussion Starters

The Discussion Starters are designed to help people think about how God speaks to us, how we speak to Him and how knowing more of who God is helps us to relate to Him. For Discussion Starter 1 you should encourage the group to recognise that God does speak in different ways, through other people, through creation, through ideas that come to us, as well as directly through Scripture. If a sense emerges that the group sees some methods of hearing from God (eg an audible voice) as somehow more significant than others, you may need to point out that Scripture itself portrays God speaking in different ways. As long as it is clear that what is heard is really from God (a good test of that is that it is fully in accord with Scripture), all these ways are equally significant. In Discussion Starter 2 it may be helpful to ask how the leaders of the churches the group belongs to are addressed and whether this has any impact on the life of the church. In Discussion Starter 3 you may like to encourage discussion of whether, and if so why, calling God by His name makes the group members feel uncomfortable; and whether or why they think it might make God feel uncomfortable or otherwise.

As a supplement to Discussion Starter 5, you might address the question of the misunderstandings that arise from concentrating solely on one aspect of God's nature (eg His lovingkindness or His judgment) and neglecting others (eg His holiness, His mercy or His passion for justice). In any prayer time at the end of the study you may find it worthwhile to encourage the group to use the things that have come out in response to Discussion Starters 4 and 5 to aid the prayers, both those for other people and those reflecting on God and your relationship with Him (praise, thanksgiving, repentance etc).

Week 2: Exclusive Rights

Opening Icebreaker

The Opening Icebreaker is intended to stimulate
discussion on the meaning of loyalty. It is clear that the
exclusive loyalty that God deserves and demands is very
different from any loyalty to a particular supermarket
chain and if comments are made about those differences,
you might like to encourage the discussion.

Aim of the Session

This session provides the opportunity for reflection on the
uniqueness of our God and the unity of the Godhead, as
well as on the necessity of absolute and exclusive loyalty.

Discussion Starters

The first three Discussion Starters provide opportunity
for further dialogue about loyalty and what it means
in relation to God. Comment on the way in which our
disloyalty affects God may emerge from the general
discussion, but if it does not it would be good for you
to bring that point out. Faith today is often assumed to
be or is seen as an optional extra; an interest or hobby
that some people get really involved in – just as football
or music might be the focus of attention for others.
Discussion Starters 4 and 5 are designed to raise questions
about this assumption. The danger of treating our service
and worship of God as a hobby, incidental to our life,
rather than the centre of all that we are and do, may be
greater than that of our serving something or someone
else instead of God.

Discussion Starter 6 should lead to talk about the nature
of the Trinity. Most groups find this difficult and tend
to avoid it. If your group looks to be heading in that
direction you might like to suggest that on another
occasion you invite one of the church leaders to come
and help the group talk it through. For Jesus, His

one-ness with God was clearly very important (cf also the prayer in John 17) and it matters that we get to grips with these concepts. Discussion Starters 7 and 8 move on to the second commandment. In some church traditions this commandment is likely to have been interpreted as referring to visual illustrations or icons used by other traditions and it may be worth following up Discussion Starter 7 with discussion of how such illustrations might be seen as helpful, as well as how they might be seen as offending against this commandment. It may also be worth including here some discussion of what the group understands as an image and the difference between images and imagery. Verbal pictures understood as metaphors illustrating certain of God's characteristics are fine; fixed depictions that limit God to our understanding of Him are not.

For Discussion Starter 8 take time to draw out the mental pictures members of the group have of God and encourage them to work out for themselves what might be helpful, or unhelpful, about those pictures. As with all the commandments it is important to consider two questions: What do other people do that might be seen as breaking these commandments? What is there in my behaviour or ideas and attitudes that might be offensive to God? Then spend time working out together what we can do about these things.

Week 3: Misrepresentation

Opening Icebreaker
The Opening Icebreaker should encourage discussion of how closely adverts relate to the item they are advertising. If it does not develop naturally you may like to direct attention to the issue of whether some kind of Trade Descriptions Act, which ensures that consumers are not deceived, is necessary or effective.

Aim of the Session
The aim of this study is to bring out the broad challenge of the third commandment and the way in which it relates to the whole of our life.

Discussion Starters
The Discussion Starters 1–4 relate to issues of offensive speech; 5–7 to issues of offensive behaviour; and the last one is more general. Make sure that the group covers one or two questions from both 1–4 and 5–7. In Discussion Starters 2 and 3 push the group into providing specific examples of ways in which they might speak positively of God – if possible with illustrations of where they have done this or heard this being done. Many Christians find this difficult and it is worthwhile spending time encouraging people to have confidence in God and in their trust in Him. If some good ideas come out in question 4, it may be worth sharing them with the church, perhaps via the website, blog and/or magazine – or any other suitable media.

The issue of people turning away from God because of the behaviour of Christians is an important one for the Church today. With Discussion Starter 5, once the initial reactions have been worked through, you might introduce the idea that people rejecting God because of the behaviour of Christians may not always be a negative thing. If Christians have conveyed the right impression of God and are genuinely imaging Jesus then the turning away may actually be related to the teaching of the cross being offensive or a refusal to accept the demands God makes (cf Paul's teaching in 1 Cor. 1:18–25). However if the real issue is that God has been misrepresented, which is probably more often the case, then that is serious. For Discussion Starter 6, it may be worth including ideas of what would be included if we had a Christian Trade Descriptions Act and whether or not we would be likely to be found guilty. In either 5 or 6 it may also be worth raising the possibility of people misrepresenting God by using phrases like 'the Lord told me ...' to support ideas when the evidence for divine provenance is very slight or non-existent.

If this really is a crucial commandment, then finding ways to help us keep it is also very significant. The prayer designed within Discussion Starter 7 could make a real difference here. If the group does find this helpful, again it could be very valuable to share this with the wider church fellowship. In fact, a sheet of collected inspirations from this whole series could be gathered together and either printed out with the Sunday news sheet or swapped with similar sheets from other groups so as to learn from each other. Discussion Starter 8 considers the nature of the Ten Commandments as a summary and how much the different elements overlap and reinforce each other.

If your study concludes with a prayer time you might like to include the Lord's Prayer this week; think particularly about what we are thinking about when we pray that God's name might be 'hallowed'.

Week 4: Respect!

Opening Icebreaker

Like the fifth commandment, the Opening Icebreaker deals with respect for people. However it is also intended to raise questions about respect in general and should therefore have relevance also to the discussion of the Sabbath. If everyone selects the same kind of characteristic considered worthy of respect (there may be a concentration of virtues, like kindness; of skills, like being able to play the piano; or status, like holding down a good job) then ask the group members to discuss why they think this is. Do they think that the characteristics they've picked out would be the same as, or different from, characteristics chosen by a secular group?

Aim of the Session

The aim of this study is to consider not just what Sabbath-keeping and parent-honouring mean in terms of behaviour, but also in terms of motivation and consequences.

Discussion Starters

The first four Discussion Starters relate to respecting the Sabbath and the last four to respecting parents – again make sure that the group considers at least one from each section. Discussion Starter 1 should lead to some discussion about what exactly is meant by observing the Sabbath day. It's worth pointing out that the Early Church deliberately chose Sunday as their day to meet together for worship, knowing very well that this was not the appointed Sabbath day. It may be helpful to ask what the group thinks might have been the reason for that. For Discussion Starter 2, the group could be asked to reflect on how important the concept of 'rest' is in the Bible and to think about whether it is undervalued or overvalued today. The question as to whether 'rest' and 'leisure' are the same thing could also be considered here. In groups of older people, some will have been brought up with very fixed ideas about this and others will have reacted against those ideas. It may be helpful to encourage discussion of how far cultural pressures affected thinking from both sides – and have sometimes stopped people from looking at what the Bible actually says. For example, does the Bible actually say that swimming, gardening or playing cricket are not permitted and, if it doesn't, does that mean anything is allowed? Younger groups have probably never really thought about it and it will be helpful for them to think through how much they are losing out if they do not take this commandment seriously.

A further line of discussion could consider whether at some stage we should take time out from virtually everything we see as essential to our everyday life: eg emails, computer games or reading, as well as what we see as our work.

As to what is involved in respecting parents, once again groups may have very fixed ideas. It is worth spending time considering how the views of different age-groups might differ and whether that is important. What is crucial, however, is to make sure that there is proper consideration of how this affects the behaviour of the people in the group. It would be very easy to get sidelined into discussing how other people do not behave in the way that we think might be appropriate. Discussion Starters 7 and 8 might bring out things that the group might, once again, consider worth sharing with the rest of the church. Discussion Starter 8 raises the question of whether sometimes either parents or children use this commandment as a justification for making unreasonable demands or as an excuse for avoiding other responsibilities. It would be good to point out that the fifth commandment is addressed to the children, rather than to the parents, and was never intended as a weapon to be used to create guilt.

Week 5: Sex and Violence

Opening Icebreaker

The Opening Icebreaker is designed to help us understand how we would feel if we were deprived of things that belonged to us – encourage the group to think more broadly here than just in terms of possessions – and therefore to create an empathy with others who have suffered the losses involved with killing, adultery and theft. This study looks at three different commandments and therefore the amount of detail able to be covered is inevitably going to be limited. Ñevertheless, it would be good if some time could be spent on each of the three areas involved.

Aim of the Session

The aim of this study is to encourage the group to think of commandments six to eight in terms of taking something from someone else that we do not have the right to take. The concentration should not be on how wicked the (other) people who do these things are, but on how far we are responsible: not just for our own behaviour (although of course that is important), but also for what is tolerated within our society. Our response should not just be 'How dreadful!' but 'What action can we take to change this?'

Discussion Starters

There are three Discussion Starters related to each individual commandment. Discussion Starters 1, 4 and 7 may be covered fairly quickly but the others are likely to take more time. Some of them deal with fairly large issues of society, some with the church and some with more personal aspects of life. Encourage the group to take seriously their own responsibility for each of these areas and to think through the actions they can take to change things. It is very easy for us to seek to avoid that responsibility by assuming the stance: 'That is all about politics and therefore nothing to do with me.' The Ten Commandments themselves, placed in the context of how life is to be lived within a society, don't allow us to take that view. Wherever it is possible, being specific about suggestions or conclusions will be helpful.

The comments made in relation to Week 1 (about the centrality of our relationship with God and the importance of recognising exactly who He is) are very relevant here. Within the discussions, try to bring the focus back to what it is about God Himself that makes Him consider these things to be so important as to be included in this key summary of the Law. Jesus' attitude to the woman taken in adultery (see the comments on Seeing Jesus in the Scripture) is probably the best guide to work through the implications of Discussion Starter 10.

Week 6: Who Are You Kidding?

Opening Icebreaker

Wrap up enough small gifts for each person in the group, making sure that some gifts might be seen as more desirable or valuable than others. Place numbers in a box for people to pick a number to determine the order in which they will select their gift. Let everyone in turn select and open a gift. However, as each person opens their gift they may swap their gift for one already opened – but no consultation with the previous owner is permitted! This means that the first person has no choice at all and the last person can pick any one of the gifts already opened.

This Opening Icebreaker provides the opportunity to want and to take something 'belonging' to someone else. It is likely that some people, even in a game situation, will be wary of doing this. It may be worth spending a little time discussing whether there were some who would have wanted to make a swap but felt constrained. If so, what was it that constrained them, eg pressure of wanting to be kind, or to be thought kind? For those who did swap, or who lost a gift they would have liked to keep, how did it make them feel?

Aim of the Session

The aim of this study is the exploration of issues relating to both truth and coveting, to work out what the Bible says and how it might affect us in our everyday lives. It may be helpful for some definitions of the two concepts to be available for the group to look at.

Discussion Starters

Four of the Discussion Starters are related to the ninth commandment and four to the tenth. Again it would be good if attention were paid to some from each section.

For the first four discussion starters, issues relating to the nature of truth, of trust, of deceit and of misrepresentation are all relevant. An amusing example for Discussion Starter 3 is 'The report of my death was an exaggeration' (Mark Twain). As in other studies it will be important to bring the group back at some point to thinking about the nature of God and how that does or should affect our view of things.

In this type of discussion the issue of whether it is sometimes kinder to lie may arise; for example, telling someone that they look good when it is obvious that their new outfit really does not suit them. Opinions will vary, but if this does happen it would be good to ask whether or not, for any examples given, it would be possible to find a kind way for the truth to be told.

Greed, jealousy and discontent lie at the heart of all coveting. It sometimes seems as if our whole economic system depends on the encouragement of these things that the Bible consistently sees as sinful. At some point in the reflection on the last four Discussion Starters, it would be good to ask whether or not the church (or churches) that the group members belong to has provided any teaching on this subject. Has any practical advice been given, to the older folk as well as to the young, as to how they might resist the pressures of society in this area? Discussion Starter 7 raises explicitly the issue of 'being content' that may also have come up in the discussion relating to 5 or 6. Does 'contentment' stifle ambition and, if so, is this a good or a bad thing? The Bible condemns 'selfish ambition' (Gal. 5:20; Phil. 2:3; James 3:16) but encourages striving for good (2 Cor. 13:11; 1 Thess. 5:15; 1 Tim. 4:10). Try to make sure that there is some discussion of how the balance in this area might be achieved.

Week 7: The Now Generation

Opening Icebreaker

The Opening Icebreaker should stimulate discussion of change, and prepare the group for thinking through what changes in our relationship with God have been initiated because of the life, death and resurrection of Jesus.

Aim of the Session

The aim of this final study is to set the Ten Commandments in the context of the whole Bible, and to examine the way in which the New Testament looks at the issues involved. The extra Bible readings are important in all the studies but this week it is really essential to look at a number of different passages. The list given could be seen as the minimum required. You might like to remind the group of this in the previous week and particularly encourage reading in advance.

Discussion Starters

Discussion Starters 1 and 2 deal with our understanding of the Law in general. There are a few people today who suggest that keeping the whole Old Testament Law should be made compulsory for all Christians. There were those in Paul's day who suggested the same thing. In the book of Galatians Paul shows why this view would be so wrong. It may be worth spending some time discussing that point. Legalism, that is treating the Law as if it were completely fixed and rigid rather than part of God's living Word and being more concerned with the letter than the spirit of what has been said, has been a problem throughout the Christian era. It is always easier to identify how this comes out in other people than to recognise it in ourselves, but encourage the group to try to be specific and self-critical.

Discussion Starters 5–7 are designed to raise questions about our own behaviour. Once more it is very important to encourage the group to be specific. It would be good to bring in again the question of how our understanding of who God is affects the way that we look at these matters. In every time and culture there have been things that the Bible clearly sees as offensive to God (often related to injustice of one kind or another) and yet Christians have accepted or even affirmed these things with the excuse of not wanting to be legalistic. Similarly, in every time and culture Christians have condemned certain things (often related to cultural preferences, such as dress or music) with the excuse of wanting to be obedient to God. If these issues do not come up naturally within the discussion, it would probably be helpful to raise them.

If the group has not already started to make notes about what they have learned from these studies in order to share them with other groups or with the church as a whole, maybe today would be a good time to encourage them to do that.

National Distributors

UK: (and countries not listed below)
CWR, Waverley Abbey House, Waverley Lane, Farnham, Surrey GU9 8EP. Tel: (01252) 784700
Outside UK (44) 1252 784700 Email: mail@cwr.org.uk

AUSTRALIA: KI Entertainment, Unit 21 317-321 Woodpark Road, Smithfield, New South Wales 2164.
Tel: 1 800 850 777 Fax: 02 9604 3699 Email: sales@kientertainment.com.au

CANADA: David C Cook Distribution Canada, PO Box 98, 55 Woodslee Avenue, Paris, Ontario N3L
3E5. Tel: 1800 263 2664 Email: sandi.swanson@davidccook.ca

GHANA: Challenge Enterprises of Ghana, PO Box 5723, Accra. Tel: (021) 222437/223249
Fax: (021) 226227 Email: ceg@africaonline.com.gh

HONG KONG: Cross Communications Ltd, 1/F, 562A Nathan Road, Kowloon. Tel: 2780 1188
Fax: 2770 6229 Email: cross@crosshk.com

INDIA: Crystal Communications, 10-3-18/4/1, East Marredpalli, Secunderabad – 500026, Andhra
Pradesh. Tel/Fax: (040) 27737145 Email: crystal_edwj@rediffmail.com

KENYA: Keswick Books and Gifts Ltd, PO Box 10242-00400, Nairobi. Tel: (254) 20 312639/3870125
Email: keswick@swiftkenya.com

MALAYSIA: Canaanland, No. 25 Jalan PJU 1A/41B, NZX Commercial Centre, Ara Jaya, 47301 Petaling
Jaya, Selangor. Tel: (03) 7885 0540/1/2 Fax: (03) 7885 0545 Email: info@canaanland.com.my

Salvation Book Centre (M) Sdn Bhd, 23 Jalan SS 2/64, 47300 Petaling Jaya, Selangor.
Tel: (03) 78766411/78766797 Fax: (03) 78757066/78756360 Email: info@salvationbookcentre.com

NEW ZEALAND: KI Entertainment, Unit 21 317-321 Woodpark Road, Smithfield, New South Wales
2164, Australia. Tel: 0 800 850 777 Fax: +612 9604 3699 Email: sales@kientertainment.com.au

NIGERIA: FBFM, Helen Baugh House, 96 St Finbarr's College Road, Akoka, Lagos.
Tel: (01) 7747429/4700218/825775/827264 Email: fbfm_1@yahoo.com

PHILIPPINES: OMF Literature Inc, 776 Boni Avenue, Mandaluyong City. Tel: (02) 531 2183
Fax: (02) 531 1960 Email: gloadlaon@omflit.com

SINGAPORE: Alby Commercial Enterprises Pte Ltd, 95 Kallang Avenue #04–00, AIS Industrial Building,
339420. Tel: (65) 629 27238 Fax: (65) 629 27235 Email: marketing@alby.com.sg

SOUTH AFRICA: Struik Christian Books, 80 MacKenzie Street, PO Box 1144, Cape Town 8000.
Tel: (021) 462 4360 Fax: (021) 461 3612 Email: info@struikchristianmedia.co.za

SRI LANKA: Christombu Publications (Pvt) Ltd, Bartleet House, 65 Braybrooke Place, Colombo 2.
Tel: (9411) 2421073/2447665 Email: dhanad@bartleet.com

USA: David C Cook Distribution Canada, PO Box 98, 55 Woodslee Avenue, Paris, Ontario N3L 3E5,
Canada. Tel: 1800 263 2664 Email: sandi.swanson@davidccook.ca

CWR is a Registered Charity – Number 294387
CWR is a Limited Company registered in England – Registration Number 1990308

Transforming lives

Courses and seminars

Publishing and new media

Conference facilities

CWR's vision is to enable people to experience personal transformation through applying God's Word to their lives and relationships.

Our Bible-based training and resources help people around the world to:
- Grow in their walk with God
- Understand and apply Scripture to their lives
- Resource themselves and their church
- Develop pastoral care and counselling skills
- Train for leadership
- Strengthen relationships, marriage and family life

and much more.

CWR Applying God's Word
to everyday life and relationships

CWR, Waverley Abbey House,
Waverley Lane, Farnham,
Surrey GU9 8EP, UK

Telephone: +44 (0)1252 784700
Email: info@cwr.org.uk
Website: www.cwr.org.uk

Registered Charity No 294387
Company Registration No 1990308

Our insightful writers provide daily Bible-reading notes and other resources for all ages, and our experienced course designers and presenters have gained an international reputation for excellence and effectiveness.

CWR's Training and Conference Centre in Surrey, England, provides excellent facilities in an idyllic setting - ideal for both learning and spiritual refreshment.

Dramatic new resource

Acts 13-28 - To the ends of the earth
by Christine Platt

This study guide for the second part of Acts covers Paul's three missionary journeys. See his strategy for urban evangelism and catch his pastoral heart for the fledgling first-century churches. Be challenged by the radical lifestyle of early believers and develop a heart for unreached peoples.
ISBN: 978-1-85345-592-6

The bestselling *Cover to Cover Bible Study* Series

1 Corinthians
Restoring harmony
ISBN: 978-1-85345-374-8

2 Corinthians
Growing a Spirit-filled church
ISBN: 978-1-85345-551-3

1 Timothy
Healthy churches - effective Christians
ISBN: 978-1-85345-291-8

23rd Psalm
The Lord is my shepherd
ISBN: 978-1-85345-449-3

2 Timothy and Titus
Vital Christianity
ISBN: 978-1-85345-338-0

Acts 1-12
Church on the move
ISBN: 978-1-85345-574-2

Acts 13-28
To the ends of the earth
ISBN: 978-1-85345-592-6

Ecclesiastes
Hard questions and spiritual answers
ISBN: 978-1-85345-371-7

Elijah
A man and his God
ISBN: 978-1-85345-575-9

Ephesians
Claiming your inheritance
ISBN: 978-1-85345-229-1

Esther
For such a time as this
ISBN: 978-1-85345-511-7

Fruit of the Spirit
Growing more like Jesus
ISBN: 978-1-85345-375-5

Genesis 1-11
Foundations of reality
ISBN: 978-1-85345-404-2

God's Rescue Plan
Finding God's fingerprints on human history
ISBN: 978-1-85345-294-9

Great Prayers of the Bible
Applying them to our lives today
ISBN: 978-1-85345-253-6

Hebrews
Jesus - simply the best
ISBN: 978-1-85345-337-3

Hosea
The love that never fails
ISBN: 978-1-85345-290-1

Isaiah 1-39
Prophet to the nations
ISBN: 978-1-85345-510-0

Isaiah 40-66
Prophet of restoration
ISBN: 978-1-85345-550-6

James
Faith in action
ISBN: 978-1-85345-293-2

For current prices visit www.cwr.org.uk/store

Available online or from your local Christian bookshop.

Cover to Cover Every Day
Gain deeper knowledge of the Bible

Each issue of these bimonthly daily Bible-reading notes gives
you insightful commentary on a book of the Old and New
Testaments with reflections on a psalm each weekend by
Philip Greenslade.

Enjoy contributions from two well-known authors every
two months, and over a five-year period you will be taken
through the entire Bible.

ISSN: 1744-0114
Only £2.75 each (plus p&p)
£14.95 for annual subscription (bimonthly, p&p included in UK)
£13.80 for annual email subscription
(available from www.cwr.org.uk/store)

Cover to Cover Complete
Read through the Bible chronologically

Take an exciting, year-long journey through the Bible, following events as they happened.

• See God's strategic plan of redemption unfold across the centuries
• Increase your confidence in the Bible as God's inspired message
• Come to know your heavenly Father in a deeper way

The full text of the flowing Holman Christian Standard Bible (HCSB) provides an exhilarating reading experience and is augmented by our beautiful:

• Illustrations
• Maps
• Charts
• Diagrams
• Timeline

And key Scripture verses and devotional thoughts make each day's reading more meaningful.

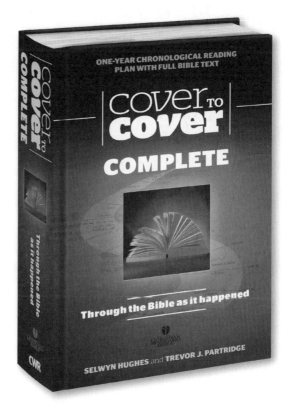